Jacksonville
in
Sesquicentennial
Retrospection
1872-1922

Volume 1

By
Larry Lydick
&
John Taylor

All proceeds from the sale of this book
are donated to the
Vanishing Texana Museum

Jacksonville
in
Retrospection

1872-2022

Copyright 2021
by
Larry Lydick & John Taylor

ISBN: 978-0-578-98912-9
Library of Congress: 2021918727
First edition, October 2021

Published by:
The Vanishing Texana Museum
& the City of Jacksonville, TX

Printed in the United States by

Christine Kjosa (Hopkins)
KJ Graphics

Correspondence and Publication requests contact:

Vanishing Texana Museum
302 South Bolton
Jacksonville, TX 75766

DEDICATIONS

This publication is dedicated to Elizabeth "Betty" Brown Ebaugh, founder, organizer, contributor, and first curator of the Vanishing Texana Museum.

The authors would also like to acknowledge the lifetime efforts of Jackson Smith, E.B. Ragsdale, and many others whose forward looking decisions and physical efforts established Jacksonville, Texas at its present location 150 years ago. It was on August 5, 1872 that the first steam engine arrived at Wilson and Main Street and Jacksonville began its future.

And, finally, we wish to thank the hundreds of local and out of town visitors that have either gifted or loaned the museum items they themselves treasured.

Foreword

This book is the result of a request by Sam Hopkins, former curator of the Vanishing Texana Museum and Chairman of the Jacksonville Sesquicentennial Committee. The compilation herein represents a short overview of fifty artifacts of the over 3000 items in the museum's collection.

The authors want to thank our docents, Jim Harris, Barry Hughes, and Helen Keller for their exceptional efforts in restoration, inventory, and patron visits to the museum.

Additionally the authors wish to thank the Board of Directors of the Vanishing Texana Museum as well as the City of Jacksonville, TX for their support in putting this publication together.

2021 Vanishing Texana Museum Board of Directors:

John Taylor (Chairperson),
Janie Barber
Barbara Hugghins
Jerry McDonald
Nancy Nesselhauf
Trina Stidham
(Director Jacksonville Public Library and
Vanishing Texana Museum)
Junior Washburn
Greg Lowe (City Secretary and advisory member)

Preface

The Vanishing Texana Museum commemorates the 150th
anniversary of the founding of Jacksonville, Texas by producing
this book of articles, artifacts, and photographs reflective of our
city's history and culture. This document serves as a companion
piece to the iconic book published by the Jacksonville Centennial
Corporation in 1972. This is not an attempt to duplicate historic
and family information from the 1972 edition, but rather to
supplement with both recent research and fifty years of hindsight
and perspective. Hopefully, then, the reader will value this volume
as an important resource in better understanding and appreciating
our town's story. It is our position that a museum should be more
than a static storehouse of items, but rather ought to combine
research with writing. This book attempts to illustrate that aspect
of the Vanishing Texana Museum. A patron once commented that
our museum was a depository of "precious memories." Our wish is
that this publication reflects that spirit and meets those criteria.

We, the curator and VTM Board of Directors, are proud of this
East Texas piney wood town and are equally thankful that we had
the opportunity to participate in Jacksonville's 2022 celebration.

Larry Lydick   John Taylor

Table of Contents

Table of Contents

The First Fifty

Sam Houston Coverlet
Circa 1836

The Sam Houston Coverlet

This handmade cotton on wool coverlet was produced before 1836. It was woven by a Mrs. Hall, the grandmother of Mrs. E.P. Dolan, Jr., who donated the piece to the Vanishing Texana Museum. Sam Houston slept beneath this coverlet while a guest in the Hall home.

By definition, coverlets are woven bed covers used as the topmost covering on a bed. The accompanying pattern was woven in as part of the process. While a quilt is produced from previously existing cloth, coverlets are made from scratch using thread spun on a spinning wheel. There were two types of coverlets: geometric and "figured fancy".

Our Houston coverlet is geometric. The patterns in figured and fancy coverlets are curvilinear and realistic and can include floral, animal, architectural and other motifs. These are the coverlets that most often contain inscriptions. Inscriptions can include the weaver's name, his location, the year it was made, the name of the person it was made for, and sometimes a slogan of some sort. In early pieces, such as our Houston coverlet, the cotton was usually left undyed. Coverlets are also reversible, unlike quilts.

In coverlet assembly, both warp and weft are made of undyed cotton. Warp and weft refer to the orientation of woven fabric. The warp direction refers to the threads that run the length of the fabric. The weft refers to the yarns that are pulled and inserted perpendicularly to the warp yarns across the width of the fabric. Small, diamond-like geometric designs of blue wool were added throughout.

The complete coverlet is 98 inches long and 75 inches wide. Because the small size of the loom limited the width, two pieces were stitched together length wise to create the final product.

Bone Family Bell
Circa 1846

Bone Bell

In 1864, John A. Rumsey, together with his brother and another partner form the Seneca Falls Pump and Fire Engine Company in Seneca, NY. They manufactured a variety of products for farming, railroads, and fire departments. A financial article about the company described it as being, "Built upon the sure foundation of meritorious goods, honorable conduct and just dealings, its growth has been as substantial as phenomenal, and its high standing is fixed as the triumph of industry, of energy and of the exercise of correct business principles." Markets can quickly change; Rumsey & Company did well until the Great Depression. It managed to hold on until 1942 when it declared bankruptcy.

The Rumsey bell on display in our outdoor exhibit is a Number 6 1/2, cast in 1899, is 27 inches in diameter, and weighs 210 pounds. The advertisement for the bell includes a column for selection of the "cipher." Although we are not sure, it appears that the British used the word cipher to mean a certain sound. The cipher for our bell is "Jaunt."

A catalog page describes this series of bell as "....represents our Steel-Amalgam Bell as we mount the larger sizes for churches, factories, semi- naries, and engine houses." Before the 911 emergency number system, bells were the main means of alerting people to emergencies and an- nouncements. Church bells had a deep, richer tone. School bells were cast using a thinner material, so they had were more "dingy" in their sound. That way the local population would not confuse school or church bells with those calling for community action.

Our Ramsey bell comes to us from the family of Dr. R.D. Bone. Sometime in the 1880's Doctor Bone purchased it for installation at the First Presbyterian Church of Larissa, TX. In early 2019 the bell was moved to the out- door display area of the museum. The bell sits atop a custom structure. There is a rope to pull, cut at adult height, to facilitate ringing of the bell.

**Kentucky Long Rifle
Circa 1847**

The Widow Maker

Visitors are always drawn to the Kentucky long rifle on display in the museum. There is no mistaking it. The rifle is approximately 62" long with a 46" barrel. It has an octagonal shaped barrel with a lead wrap at the end. The initials "JO" are stamped on the barrel. The hammer, lock plate, and trigger mechanism are adorned with two pheasants behind the hammer and the words "Henry Parker Warranted" marked on the front of the hammer. Not much is known about Mr. Parker except that he lived and worked producing trigger lock mechanisms for long rifles in New Jersey area and died in the 1850's.

Immigrants from Germany and Switzerland clustered in the Lancaster, PA area. Lead shot for hunting was expensive, so their first innovation was to reduce the caliber for a new weapon design. Next, they added 10 inches of length to the barrel, then added a spiral grooving inside the barrel. These new rifles were deadly at 200 yards, an unheard of range for its day. A Kentucky rifle was individually made by a local gunsmith. He would harvest a hard wood, and then purchase mechanisms from outside vendors. Barrels were generally forged by the gunsmith himself. They were built one at a time and so comes the expression "lock, stock, and barrel."

So how did these rifles, developed in Pennsylvania, become known as Kentucky rifles? One of the most famous people of the day was Daniel Boone, a Kentuckian, who was always seen carrying a long rifle. It is reported that Mr. Boone carried a long rifle through the Cumberland Gap as he opened America to western expansion. It was this association with Daniel Boone and his home state of Kentucky that led people to call any long rifle a Kentucky rifle.

"From a flat bar of soft iron, hand-forged into a gun barrel; laboriously bored and rifled with crude tools, fitted with a stock hewn from a maple tree in the neighboring forest, and supplied with a lock hammered to shape on the anvil; an unknown smith, in a shop long silent, fashioned a rifle which changed the whole course of world history, made possible the settlement of a continent, and ultimately freed our country of foreign domination." So writes Captain Jon G. W. Dillin in the dedication of his 1924 book, The Kentucky Rifle.

Spinning Wheel made by Mr. Benge
Circa 1850

Mr. Benge's Wheel

Our spinning wheel was handmade of pine and oak lumber by George C. Benge in 1850 and was presented to his daughter, Mrs. Matilda Benge Earle, in 1851. The daughter was the mother of Amada Earl Grey of Jacksonville. Thread was spun on this wheel to make blankets, spreads, Linsey dresses, and for making clothes for many soldiers during the Civil War.

They raised sheep, sheared them by hand using tools on display in the museum, then sent the wool by horseback to Larissa (near Mt. Selman) to a "carder" who carded the wool into rolls for them. They then spun the rolls of wool into thread using spinning wheels. Once complete, the ladies would then take the thread on horseback to Amada Love's house (a neighbor) to dye, using local plants, in her copper kettle. The copper kettle would produce brighter colors when dying the thread. The most popular colors were red (made from Cochineal bugs) and Indigo Blue (from Indigo weed) and brown (from green walnut hulls).

Our spinning wheel was used as a working model by a Mrs. Foster to illustrate spinning during the Jacksonville Golden Jubilee in 1922.

A coverlet, using thread spun on this wheel, is on display in the museum.

Mr. Rhome did not leave instructions for opening his safe. Turns out the safe can only be opened by using a hobnail disguised as part of the safe's construction. The nail portion of the hobnail is pressed into a small hole in the front of the safe. This releases a door that accesses a keyhole. Mr. Rhome's safe had several loose hobnails that frustrated our attempts to open it. It remained secured until 2018 when a 10-year-old visitor figured it out in about 15 minutes!

Mr. Roan's Safe
Circa 1855

A Hob Nail Safe

On display in your Vanishing Texana Museum is one of the first types of metal safes to be manufactured in the United States. They were called Hobnail safes. Pieces of sheet iron were fashioned around a wooden chest selected by the customer. A blacksmith would then fit straps of metal banding over the sheet iron. Cast iron nails with oversized heads were then pushed through the heated metal banding giving the safe a "hobnail" appearance and exceptional security from break-ins.

Our safe was owned by Pete Gremps Rhome (1806 – 1875), one of the earliest and most colorful residents of Old Jacksonville. Mr. Rhome arrived in Old Jacksonville in 1854. His arrival was big news as he brought with him brand new mercantile stock said to have been purchased in New York City. The material was shipped to Houston via Galveston then hauled from Houston via oxen wagons to Old Jacksonville, probably a six-week journey. At that time safes were only manufactured in the northeast, so it is most likely that he purchased it in New York to protect his papers, documents, titles, and money during the voyage and final delivery to Old Jacksonville.

In 1855 Mr. Rhome purchased the inventory and existing business of James L. Warren located on the north end of the square in Old Jacksonville. He continued to operate his business at that location until the Civil War. During the Civil War there were neither enough people nor inventory to keep the business operating. It would be more than a year after the end of the war before he could reopen his store. He moved his business to new Jacksonville when it was established in 1872. Although he moved his firm to the new town, he continued to live in Old Jacksonville and commuted daily until his death. Later, fire destroyed his old home when other buildings in the old town also burned.

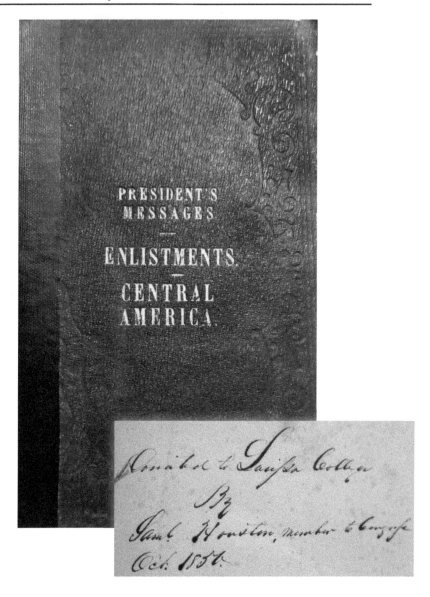

Providing historic context, Houston would soon be elected Governor of Texas. Because of his opposition to secession from the Union, he was removed from office by the state legislature and would die in Huntsville before the Civil War ended.

President's Messages 1856

The President's Messages

Complementing the museum's Houston coverlet, which Sam Houston napped under, is a rare and surprising discovery. A US Senate publication by the 34th Congress, first session, entitled *President's Messages: Enlistments, Central America* (published in 1856, by the US Senate), was gifted to Larissa College in 1856. Larissa College was located between what is now Jacksonville and Bullard, Texas, and was one of the premier educational facilities in Texas prior to the Civil War. The book was rediscovered several years ago among the museum's collection and upon examination revealed a dedication in Houston's own hand, reading, "Donated to Larissa College by Sam Houston, member of Congress, Oct., 1856." This inscription was probably made with an eagle feather quill, Sam Houston's pen of choice. Authenticity of the signature has been given by the Sam Houston Memorial Museum in Huntsville, Texas.

The dark brown book itself contains correspondence between representatives of the United States and Great Britain regarding the British habit of enlisting US citizens as British soldiers while on American territory. The book, assembled by then President Franklin Pierce, is a series of letters and interviews with both nations' principals, primarily James Buchannan, our next president, and the British Foreign Secretary. In addition, another section presents similar documents concerning the subject of perceived nefarious British activities in Central America. Ten thousand copies of the book were printed.

McKee's Grist Wheel
Circa 1857

McKee's Grist Wheel

On display in our outdoor museum is a grist wheel from McKee's Mill. It is one of the last vestiges of one of the area's earliest industries and one that was a genuine necessity for a pioneer community. Water powered mills in these pioneer communities ground corn, wheat, and other food products for local families as well as their livestock. They also provided power to run sawmills to build homes, barns, business buildings, churches, and other structures. In our history of early Jacksonville you might note that we talk about log structures, like the first hotel or Jackson Smith's blacksmith shop, because the mills for sawing and planning were not yet built.

J.W. McKee built a water powered mill for lumber and food processing at Larissa on what would become known as Killough Creek in 1872. McKee came to the area from Tennessee with the McKee Expedition in which several families immigrated to our part of East Texas. Killough Creek was fed by a large spring, still active today, and known for its large and constant supply of fresh, healthy water. Nat McCormick, a tradesman and experienced user of a slide rule, engineered the huge power wheel on display as well as the mill structure itself.

The McKee Mill also ground wheat and corn as well as operating a carding machine which prepared cotton raised on local farms for weaving in the days when pioneers made their own clothes, bedding and other necessities. Corn was a primary crop for farmers in both early and the new Jacksonville community. Corn shellers, like the working model in the museum on loan from Junior Washburn, were used to remove the corn kernels from the cob. The dried kernels were then taken to the mill where they were ground into corn meal for use in baking and other purposes.

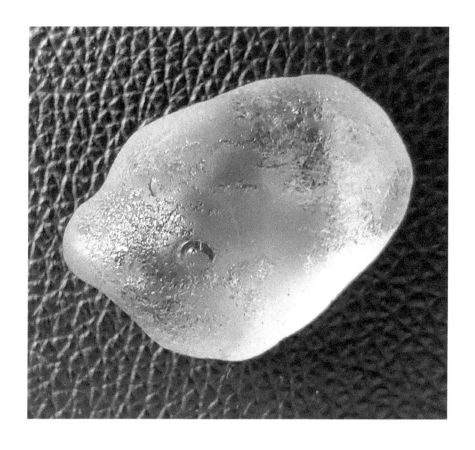

**Doctor Noell's Madstone
Circa 1857**

The Noell Madstone of Cherokee County

B efore France's Louis Pasteur developed an inoculation for rabies in 1885, a "Madstone" was the only medical option for treatment. Dr. Noell (1818-1901) brought his madstone to Alto, Texas from Virginia in 1860. Madstones are concretions formed in the stomachs of cudchewing mammals, the animal of choice being the deer. The stone would be boiled in milk and applied to the affected area where it adhered and would "draw" toxic material from the wound, eventually turning the stone green! The artifact itself is unique in that it is crystal like in appearance and displays a shiny, smooth, translucent surface. It measures one and a quarter inches in length and two in diameter. It is a beauty to behold!

This stone treated thousands of patients over the years. Eighty-one patients were documented in a journal kept by Dr. Noell's daughter, Miss Fanny Noell, from 1900 to 1903. That journal is on display at the VT Museum. Miss Noell moved to Jacksonville in the 1920s, bringing the story of the stone with her. The Noell madstone is the best documented stone of its kind in Texas. It passed down to John Tom Ahearn, and then his son Dr. Michael Ahearn, both from Jacksonville. The last known person known to be treated was Dr. Hogan Stripling, founder of Jacksonville's Stripling Clinic.

This unusual artifact remains an important and interesting part of Cherokee County medical history.

Union Army Civil War Era Canteen
Circa 1862

Civil War Canteen

Initially the Vanishing Texana Museum staff assumed this canteen was of WWI vintage, but research revealed it was from the Civil War period.

Over all, the canteen is in superb condition. It is eight inches in diameter and three inches wide, holding three pints of liquid. The cover is entirely intact, and bears a large "U.S." across the center. The rolled pewter spout has the original cork stopper with a connecting chain. Some of the leather carrying strap with metal buckle is also present.

The US government first issued this style canteen in 1857. It has a sharp edge where the two semi-spherical plates were soldered together. This canteen was less bulky than earlier models and included a cloth cover. The covers varied in color from grey to blue, but mellowed to brown (as is our example) over time. The bottom half of the cover was sewn by machine while the upper section was completed by hand. No stamps or inscriptions are present, though it is thought to have been produced in New York State between 1861 and 1862. Northern canteens were shipped to Union troops in boxes of 200, and the original cost was from ten to seventeen cents each.

This canteen was an excellent product, carefully conceived, and one that the Confederacy could not replicate due to a lack of manufacturing centers. Perhaps a former Confederate soldier liberated this canteen from a captured Union soldier, brought it back to the Jacksonville area where it remained until gifted to the Vanishing Texana Museum.

Lucy Holcombe Pickens - 1865

In addition, there is an East Texas connection in the Picken's story. Cherokee County from Alto, to Rusk, to Jacksonville is laced with Holcombs, and yes, both branches are each descended from brothers William (born about 1645) and Richard Holcombe.

Queen of the South

The first historic female to appear on paper money was Lucy Holcombe Pickens (1832-1899). Her image was not placed on US bills, however, but Confederate ones instead. Born in Tennessee, the family moved near Marshall, Texas when she was fourteen. Due to her father, Beverly Holcombe, suffering heavy losses on a horse race, the ambitious Lucy was encouraged to marry young and well.

Widowed Colonel Francis W. Pickens, a man twice her age, was found suitable and they married shortly after Pickens was appointed US Ambassador to Russia in 1858. The youthful Lucy Pickens became a court favorite due to her quick wit, beauty, and gift for French and Russian. Czar Alexander II even became the Godfather to their child!

Returning to South Carolina, Francis Pickens was elected governor several days before the state seceded from the Union. Mrs. Pickens becomes the stereotypical Southern belle, and contributed generously to a local militia which resulted in a unit being named after her: The Holcombe Brigade. Lucy was further honored by having her image embossed on several denominations of Confederate currency, to include three issues of $100 bills and one issue of a $1 note. Our museum has two examples of these.

During the war Lucy was often referred to as the Queen of the South. However, in 1869, her husband died and with the war's end so had her popularity.

The legacy of Lucy Holcombe Pickens continues. Her sculptured bust resides in the University of South Carolina library. Also, it is claimed by some that she invented "iced tea" as an alternative to the Mint Julip! Perhaps her greatest legacy, though, is that author Margaret Mitchell modeled her character Scarlet O'Hara in *Gone with the Wind* after Lucy Pickens!

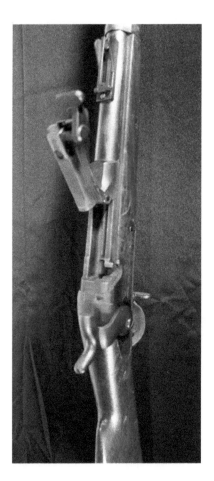

US Army Springfield Rifle, Model 1873
Circa 1874

Trapdoor Rifle

The link between Jacksonville, Texas and this iconic rifle is interesting. In the early years following Jacksonville's founding in 1872, the bustling settlement was rough and somewhat lawless. Law enforcement officers were few in number. The potential for bank robbery inspired the First National Bank (now the Austin Bank) to give Springfield rifles to several merchants surrounding the bank near the intersection of Commerce and Main streets. In case of a bank robbery, it was hoped the merchants would produce their weapons and protect the bank! The Vanishing Texana Museum's Springfield was the one given to the Ragsdale Brothers' Store in 1902.

The Springfield, Model 1873, has a remarkable history and story. It was the first breech-loading weapon adopted by the US Army and came in both carbine and full-length versions. Troops referred to the 1873 Model as the "Trapdoor" Springfield as the single cartridge was placed into an open breech resembling a trapdoor. The weapon was also known for its powerful kick. The museum's rifle is marked with serial number 271943, and the stock is stamped 1873. It was one of the finest weapons then available.

Fame was achieved by the Springfield, 1873 model, with its success during the series of Indian Wars fought after the Civil War. It also was Apache chief Geronimo's weapon of choice! Eleven to twelve rounds of cartridge .45-70-405 could be fired per minute.

However, this model was not perfect. The troops of General Custer carried the carbine version into the Battle of the Little Bighorn. The copper shell casings jammed (later to be replaced by brass) and black powder smoke easily revealed location, and this perhaps had some contribution to the battle's outcome.

The Army used the 1873 Springfield for twenty years. It was replaced due to the development of bolt action rifles utilizing multiple cartridge magazines and other innovations.

The Vanishing Texana Museum has a modest number of weapons on display, but each one has a story to tell. Come and hear the story!

Peach Peeler
Circa 1878

PEACH ORCHARD, JACKSONVILLE, TEXAS.

1934 - Jacksonville ships 1000 carloads of peaches

A Peach Peeler

Although Jacksonville is best known for its tomatoes, the first successful fruit crop in the area was peaches. They were so popular that no home would want to be without a peach peeler like the one on display in the museum.

The climate and soil around Jacksonville are perfect for growing peaches. Even before immigrants, Indians raised peaches. The commercial peach industry had its beginnings as an educational project at Larissa College championed by the school's president Dr. F.L.Yoakum. When the Civil War took all of his students, Dr. Yoakum continued to experiment with the trees with the goal of improving taste, size, and resistance to disease. In the 1870's he opens his nursery with his sons peddling the trees to farmers in the area. A Cumberland Presbyterian minister, N.A. Davis, was so impressed with the trees and their fruit, that he plants an orchard of Elberta peaches to supplement his income. One of his employees, John Wesley Love, saves his earnings and plants his own orchard which eventually covers over 600 acres located on the grounds of what is now Love's Lookout Park. From his orchards, over 100 carloads of peaches were shipped via the Cotton Belt Railroad to anxiously awaiting customers on the east coast.

There are lots of ways to peel a peach, but the peeler manufactured by the Sinclair Scott Company was the most popular in the early 1900's. Jacksonville. Peach peelers differ from apple peelers. The most notable is how it holds the peach. Apples are held onto the peeler by a spike mechanism which holds the apple while a razor like device removes the apple skin. Our peeler has three spring loaded prongs that fit over the peach pit. A small rounded anvil, or guide, then gently rests against the soft skin of a peach. A cup shaped blade is then spun rotationally to slice the skin off the rotating peach, leaving it perfectly intact for use in your favorite pie, cobbler, or just to eat.

Match Box
Circa 1879

The Barber Match Company

One of the items visitors always comment on in is a colorful box labeled "Race Matches." The distinctively lithographed front panel on the box depicts the images of five women of different races: Indian, Negro, Caucasian, Mongolian, and Malay. The advertising text reads, "5 Races, 5 colors, 5 cents." With the advent of the telegraph, the world of the late 1800's seemed to shrink and there was a keen interest in anything exotic. The match crate seems to be drawing upon that interest. Additional information on the front of the crate includes the name of the manufacturer, Barber Match Company, that the iron crate itself was patented in 1879, and that the product, patented in 1870, was a "Centennial Medal Winner." The crate was used as the shipping crate as well as a table top display and product storage case.

In 1847 the Barber Match Company was formed with its founders, George and Eliz Barber making matches by hand. By 1860, there were over 75 match manufactures in the United States and the industry was about to enter a period of mechanization and consolidation. In December, 1880 the Barber Match Company and eleven other companies merged into the Diamond Match Company which is still in operation today. Match manufacturing was a dangerous and unhealthy business. Poorly paid workers often developed phosphorus necrosis, also known as Phossy's Jaw. The Diamond Match Company was able to formulate a new blend of chemicals that led to the production of the first non-poisonous match. As a humanitarian gesture, and at the request of President Howard Taft, it agreed to forfeit all patent rights allowing rival companies to cheaply switch to non-poisonous match production. Still, Diamond Match maintained its industry leadership by turning out 250 million matches a day by 1911.

Mr. Morris' Trees Planted 1883

Mr. Morris and his Magnolia Trees

In 1872, as part of the creation of our new town, the International and Great Northern Railroad dedicated a "Public Square" in the center of town. Although the city has geographically meandered about in its growth, the square has remained, but today we know it as the "City Park," or the Hazel Tilton Park, that is bordered by Highway 79, South Bolton St., Larissa St., and Main St.

In 1889, a local resident, Mr. H.L. Morris, proposed that the park be filled with Magnolia Trees. In the spring of 1890, the city council agreed and, under Mr. Morris' supervision, dozens of trees were planted.

So, what happened to all the Magnolia Trees that used to be in the park? Some were lost when a city water tower was constructed to service the steam engines of the Texas and New Orleans Railroad. Construction of the old band pavilion might have taken a tree or two. Others fell to the right-of-way stolen by the Cotton Belt Railroad, which ran on a diagonal line through the park, a scar still visible today. The Jacksonville Public Library, completed in 1940, took a few more. Construction of the City Fire Station and the Cherokee County War Memorial just about finished off the last of the trees that were planted in the 1800's. One remained on the grounds of the museum, but it fell ill about two years ago and had to be felled.

Still, one remains and it is a magnificent tree! It sits on the corner of Highway 79 and Main Street, in front of the fire station. The trunk of the tree shows many scars as it has fought to withstand the test of time. Using the adjacent street light poles as a guide, we estimate it to be about 50' high. If you are in a car, you'll need to be looking for it before you get to the fire station to appreciate its full beauty.

Mr. Aber's Brick 1890

Mr. Aber's Brick

One of the most surprising items in the museum's collection is a brick manufactured by the Aber Brick and Basket Company of Jacksonville.

Ed Aber was born in Seneca, NY in 1852. He married Susan Katherine Haberle in 1874 when he was manufacturing furniture. An epidemic broke out and soon demand for his services turned to making coffins. To escape the epidemic, Ed moved his family to East Texas. Before settling in Jacksonville, Ed visited a company that was unsuccessfully attempting to make baskets. Ed figured out how to do it using local sweetgum trees. In 1890, Ed moves his family to Jackson- ville. His wife's family also moves here and eventually, together, they purchase two lots on South Bolton Street. Ed erects a saw mill and brick making kiln to build homes that are still standing. Close by, on Deveraux Street, Ed organizes the Aber businesses that will eventually make fruit boxes, baskets, wood molding, turned wood, and bricks. Ed moves on, selling the brick and basket business to his Haberle relatives.

The swastika symbol chosen by Mr. Aber was used by many cultures throughout the past 3,000 years to represent life, sun, power, strength and good luck. Even in the early twentieth century, the swastika was still a symbol with positive connotations and often found on items like coins and building facades. Native American tribes, particularly those in the Southwest, also incorporated the design into their culture: Hopi and Navajo referred to it as 'The Whirling Logs of Healing." The term swastika itself is derived from Sanskrit su (good) + asti (it is) + suffix ka (soul). During the times that Aber kilnfired this brick, the symbol had a surge of popularity in the Western world after it was discovered during the excavation of the ancient city of Troy.

31

Washing Machines 1891

Wash Day

Many artifacts were considered labor-saving but by today's standards are considered labor-intensive. Our new washboard exhibit is an example of this. The exhibit includes a National Washboard, a Flyer Brass Board, a child's glass framed washboard, and even a "washing machine" manufactured in the late 1800's.

There is no recorded inventor of the washboard, but we do know that in 1797 a Mr. James King received a patent for a "hand powered wash board." Later, in 1837, a Mr. Stephen Rust received a patent for the "rippled surface" that is found on almost every washboard still around. Mass production of washboards coincided with the Industrial Revolution when a 19 year old named Edward Kemp opened a screen door manufacturing business in 1884. It wasn't until 1891 that the product line was expanded to include washboards and Kemp moved his business to Chicago where he forms a partnership with Sears-Roebuck. The Sears relationship provides Kemp with the capital to purchase competitors and consolidate his hold on the market. Kemp dies unexpectedly in 1916, but his business partners run the businesses into the 1970's.

Initially, zinc and later galvanized metal is used for the washing surface. The Flyer Brass board in our collection was marketed as an upgrade to those metals, as brass did not rust and was thought to be more durable than galvanized. Glass took over during World War II.

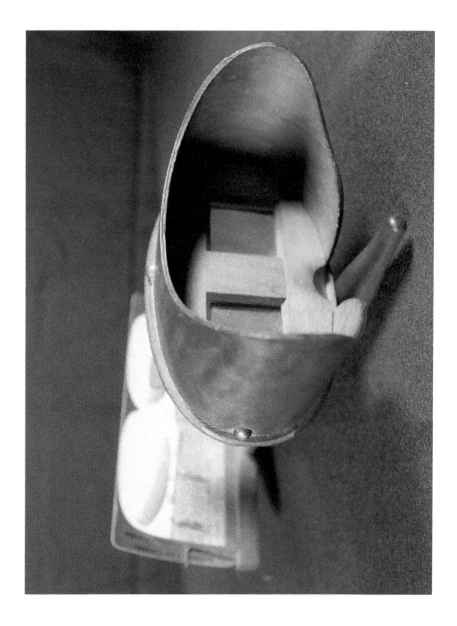

Stereoscopic Viewer 1895

The Stereoscopic Viewer

The Vanishing Texana Museum has several vintage stereoscopic viewers accompanied by dozens of antique viewing cards. When the library was located where the museum is currently, the viewers and slides were kept out on an old library table ready for instant use by patrons both young and old.

The concept was to employ a camera with two lenses, each set about 2.5 inches apart- the equivalent of space between human eyes. When the two images were placed on cards and viewed through a designed scope, a three-dimensional effect was achieved.

Early versions of the viewer were expensive and cumbersome. However, America's own Oliver Wendell Holmes (1809-1875) - doctor, poet, inventor- developed a less expensive handheld viewer that won the American market. Several models of the Holmes stereoscope viewer are displayed in the museum made by different companies, such as The Perfecscope by the H. C. White Company (1895 patent), and The Saturn Scope developed by James V. Davis (1895/6 patent).

The museum's photo cards date to the 1920s and depict a wedding, World War I battle scenes and various exotic locations. The cards were 3.5 by 7 inches, slightly bowed to fit a slide holder, and made of thick cardboard. Usually there was a lengthy descriptive narrative on the reverse telling the story of the photo. In 1904, the Keystone View Company (1882-1963) of Meadville, Pennsylvania emerged as the leading world producer of stereo photos which were sold in sets of 75, 100, 200, and 300.

Leslie's Dominos 1897

Dominos

*Of course, I have played outdoor games.
I once played dominoes in an open-air cafe in Paris.*
- Oscar Wilde

This historical item is simply a set of dominos. They are stored in an exquisite dovetailed wooden case with a sliding cover. Scrawled in pencil on the reverse side of the cover in child-like writing is "Leslie Xmas, 1895".

It is generally believed that Christian missionaries brought the game from China back to Italy in the early 1700's. From there it quickly spread across Europe becoming the most popular parlor and pub game of the time. The word "Domino" is French for a black and white hood worn by Christian priests in winter, which is probably where the name of the game is derived from. From England the game voyaged across the ocean to the colonies and eventually to Leslie's home in Jacksonville, TX. Leslie's dominos were probably purchased at a local merchant by her parents. Perhaps they visited the Brown Dixon Mercantile Store or one of Jacksonville's other merchants along Commerce Street.

Her dominos are constructed from bone with a double ebony wood backing. The ebony wood backing prevented your opponents from seeing the dominos in your hand. The two parts are secured together by a brass pin called a spinner. The pin protrudes slightly above the surface of the playing side.

Sooo...did Leslie play dominos or 42? It seems that 42 was conceived in Garner, TX, a small town west of Fort Worth. It was there that two boys, William A. Thomas and Walter Earl, reportedly "invented" the domino game 42. William, age 12, and Walter, age 14, were children of devout Baptists and were caught playing cards. The two boys did not want to give up their pastime and so set out to find a way to play cards using dominos. By the fall of 1887, they had devised a four-player game using double-six dominos that incorporated bidding and trumps, very similar to the game of 42 played in Texas today.

Acme Jewel Parlor Stove 1899

Acme Jewel Parlor Stove

This model 23 "parlor stove" (or "4 o'clock stove") was made at the Detroit Stove Works of Michigan in 1899. The company was founded in 1864 by brothers Jeremiah and James Dwyer. At one time Detroit was known as the "stove capital of the world."

The lavishly designed, Baroque inspired 125-pound stove used wood and was the center piece of a living room, dining room, or parlor. The stove exhibits high quality iron work and beauty of design. This model could be loaded from the side or top, accommodating twenty-three inch sticks of wood. Removing the finial and attachment exposed a cooking surface for perhaps brewing tea, coffee, or hot water to adjust room humidity. When new, the stove sold for $16.25!

Stove production increased with the realization that an open- hearth fire place used ten times the amount of fire wood as the innovative enclosed stove. Fully loaded the parlor stove could comfortably heat a room for four to six hours.

This stove is one of several museum items, such as the Victor Talking Machine and stereographic viewer that would commonly be found in Jacksonville homes from 1900 through the 1930s.

Adding Machine 1901

Adding Machines

For most of human history, the act of adding numbers together was a learned task. There were early adding devices like an abacus or even some mechanical devices invented by scientists or clockmakers, but it would take the American industrial revolution to finally produce a marketable (although generally not very reliable) adding machine. At first the designs required the user to insert a stylus into the machine to move gears and wheels. Later versions had a column of slots for each digit to be entered. The most successful of this later version was made by the American Can Company. Number 18,153 of their machines was purchased by the Brown Dixon Store in Jacksonville, TX sometime in 1913. The price then was $35.00, about $728.00 in 2017 money. The adding machine is almost cubic in shape about 9" in all directions and weighs 16 pounds. There is a brass label affixed to the front of the machine that reads, "AMERICAN ADDING MACHINE, American Can Company, Adding Machine Division, Chicago, ILL." The machine they purchased, that still works, is on display in your Vanishing Texana Museum.

The use of this machine in the Brown Dixon Store was sure to speed checkout and reduce errors, but was probably also an item of curiosity.

Smith Premier No. 2 1902

Smith – Premier No. 2

One of the first things visitors see when entering the museum is our type- writer collection. From an 1881 Blickenderfer to an Underwood used for the typing class at Jacksonville High School in 1957, there is a lot to see in this exhibit. We'll even invite you to try out a 1930's Royal portable typewriter purchased right here in Jacksonville! Kids love the mechanical sound and feel of the machine and get gleeful watching parents/ grandparents try it out.

Another typewriter tied to our community is a Smith Premier Number 2. The accession file from 1986 says it was used at the Brown Dixon store that was located on Commerce Street in the 1880's making it over 100 years old when it was gifted to the museum. On the manufacturer's mast head was a dedication of the typewriter to a man whose name we did not recognize.

Our Smith Premier No. 2 was one of the most advanced writing instruments of its day. The typewriter has no shift key to make capital letters with, but rather a separate key board devoted to capital letters. Built inside the typewriter is a round, stiff brush. Hold down the proper keys and the brush spins around cleaning off any excess ink that might have built up on the letters.

The copper band riveted to the mast head is engraved with the manufacturer's name, but to the left it said, "Presented to.. and on the right it appeared to read as, ".. J.J. Pastorien." Who was Mr. Pastorien and how did Mr. Brown end up with his typewriter?

It's a mystery we'll be happy to reveal when you visit your Vanishing Texana Museum.

Crown Bottling Works 1904

The Crown Bottling Works

Bottling in Jacksonville begins in 1896 with Ambrose Johnson
(1867-1943) who created a space at the back of his drugstore to
manufacture small bottles. Ambrose sold his business in 1904 to Harry
Tilley, also a pharmacist as well as a customer.

Harry only offers soda pop during the summer months when demand was
high, but eventually he contacts with Coca Cola to bottle and distribute
their product in Jacksonville and surrounding communities. The bottling
facility was first located in his drugstore at Main and Wilson Streets
where in 1904 he processed 25 gallons of Coke syrup. By 1908 demand
is so high that he sets up a bottling plant at 224 South Bolton. The plant
was the first building in the city to have a concrete floor. A mason, who
specialized in this new construction method, was brought in from the east
coast to oversee the pour. The new location meets the needs for increased
production, processing over 1,000 gallons annually by 1912. In 1922 the
business is incorporated as the Crown Coca Cola Bottling Company.
Frank Gordon Tilley takes over the business from his father in 1928 and
in 1937 moves the plant to its final location at Main and Nacogdoches
Streets. Windows to the production floor were part of the design and soon
local kids were lining up to watch the bottles march along the production
line. Except for the sugar shortages during World War II, business
remains strong. By 1954 the company is processing over 30,000 gallons
of Coca Cola syrup annually. Additionally the plant contracts to make
and distribute Dr. Pepper, Barqs Root Beer, and Sprite.

Harry Gordon Tilley was the last family member to run the Crown
Bottling Company. The plant closed its doors on April 15, 1988. Most
of the plant's equipment was shipped to the Coca Cola facility in Tyler.
Eventually the property was sold to the UT Health Center.

Farmer's Forge - 1906

Farmer's Forge

R ecently, your Vanishing Texana Museum was visited by a couple
from Nacogdoches. They enjoyed their tour and at the end asked
if we would be interested in an antique blacksmith forge. Given that
Jackson Smith, the founder of our community, was a blacksmith and the
first to set up in old Jacksonville, we knew it would be a perfect addition
to our collection.

As a side note, the term blacksmith derives from two functions. First,
the iron turns black as it is heated and secondly from the English term
"smite" which means "to hit."

Here in old Jacksonville, Jackson Smith's shop would have been perhaps
the most important business in town, but changes were coming and they
were coming fast. The Industrial Revolution was underway at the start of
the 1800's. Soon Jackson's customers could save money by purchasing
items they needed made by factories in the East and Upper Midwest.
Jackson's business would become basically a repair facility for the locals.
Even that segment of the business was reduced by the availability of
small forges like the one on display in the museum.

Our forge was manufactured by The Canedy Otto Manufacturing
Company of Chicago Heights, IL. In one of the largest manufacturing
plants in the Chicago area they manufactured forges, blowers, and drills.
In 1907, their #8 catalog, a 72-page publication, listing various products
and re- pair parts. On the cover was the company motto, "Quality is the
true test of cheapness." Our forge is diagramed on page 46 of the catalog.
It is listed as a "Chicago Forge Model Number 151." It is accurately
described as being 30" tall, weighing 70 pounds and marketed as being
"suitable for farms, small shops, and tool makers." The cost was $16.00
plus freight. Although it was one of the least expensive in the Canedy
Otto catalog, our donated forge is still fully operational.

Tombstone in City Cemetery

The James - Younger Gang Visits Jacksonville

This simple marker in our city cemetery ties our community to one of the most notable outlaw gangs of the 19th century. The James - Younger Gang.

The three prime founders of the gang honed their skills during the Civil War. Later the brothers in arms joined with other Confederate soldiers to become outlaws. On February 12, 1866, the group carried out one of the first daylight armed bank robberies in U.S. history when they held up the Clay County Savings Association in Liberty, Missouri. Even the Pinkerton Detective Agency was called in, but they were unable to capture the bad guys. On July 21, 1873, the gang carried out the first train robbery west of the Mississippi River, derailing a locomotive near Adair, Iowa. In addition to taking any valuables from the safe on the train, they also took to robbing the passengers.

After a botched robbery in Minnesota, Cole surrenders. Frank and Jesse escape west across Minnesota. In October, 1882 Frank surrenders to law enforcement, but is never found guilty of anything. Cole received a pardon. Together with Frank, he forms up a "Wild West Show" bringing their show to Jacksonville in February, 1907.

Their arrival in Jacksonville might have just passed into history except for an unfortunate event. A member of the band, a drummer named Jack Wallace, died suddenly. Responsibility for his remains fell to the Wild West Show. Younger sent several telegrams in an attempt to find some relative, but to no avail. Younger finally purchased a plot in the Jacksonville City Cemetery and the man was given a respectable funeral. Younger must have liked the man because he went a step further and paid for a stone marker to be placed on the grave site. No one has come forward to claim a relationship with the man buried there.

The Caboose Potbellied Stove

The Caboose Potbellied Stove

Trains define the origin, prosperity, and even history of Jacksonville, Texas. Indeed, the town's founding in 1872 only occurred because of the arrival of the train. In fact, the very land the Vanishing Texana Museum sits upon was a gift to the city by the International Railroad. Clearly, Jacksonville was initially a railroad town and for that reason this museum publication highlights an artifact that reflects the importance and presence of trains in Jacksonville.

The potbellied stove was common in mid to late nineteenth century and early twentieth century America. Usually, they were found in general stores, one room school houses, and train stations. However, an additional breed was produced exclusively for the caboose, the last car on a freight train. The caboose was provided to shelter railroad workers and they needed to be kept warm!

Our museum stove was made by the Hart Manufacturing Company of Louisville, Kentucky toward the end of the nineteenth century. It is model number A-1, made of cast iron, and stands 24 inches tall with a base 20 inches deep. Whereas other potbellied stoves were elevated on 12-inch legs, caboose stoves had no legs and for safety factors were bolted to the floor. Coal was preferred for fuel as that was what powered the train, therefore readily available. While the crew worked throughout the train, leaving the stove largely unattended, a double latch system protected each stove door from accidentally being opened by the jarring and swaying motion of the train. For additional safety, a lipped rim ran around the top of the stove preventing a coffee pot or pan from sliding off and spilling.

J.L. Brown Doll House 1909

Our Doll House

In 1909, Jacksonville businessman and philanthropist, J.L. Brown (1866-1944) gave his six-year-old daughter Elizabeth "Betty" Brown a doll house for a birthday present. That same doll house was a featured attraction at the 1972 Jacksonville Centennial celebration having been recently repaired by Mrs. George L. Barber.

J.L. Brown was the founder of Brown Department store here in Jacksonville. In addition, he was the first president of the First National Bank, and in 1922 was president of the committee in charge of planning the 50th anniversary of Jacksonville. Mr. Brown was one of the library's original founders. In property left to the City of Jacksonville in his will, funds were accessed that allowed the expansion of the library, the structure that now houses our Vanishing Texana Museum. Elizabeth, Brown's only child, became Mrs. Elizabeth Ebaugh, and eventually was president of the Jacksonville library and original curator/organizer of the museum.

The doll house is a wonder, and includes five levels with 123 windows. The structure stands fifteen inches tall to the top of the belfry tower, and is seventeen inches wide and eleven inches deep. It is constructed of heavy painted cardboard that includes a green roof and white exterior walls, all mounted on a brown wooden frame. The architectural style is a mixture of Italian (rectangular tower), German (enormous roofed area), Moorish (Arabic-shaped windows and elaborate sunscreens), English (crenellations around roof line), and Texan (large sweeping verandas). This doll house has a special place in our museum and assists in telling the story of our city. We suspect it will be on display again in 2072!

Gout Stool
Circa 1900

My Toe Hurts !

The Vanishing Texana Museum was gifted a "gout stool" by Linda Lesniewski to honor local Jacksonville physician, Dr. James Low Jr. This medical piece of furniture was produced to assist in the control of discomfort created by gout. Gout is a form of painful arthritis that affects joints, particularly in the feet and legs. Quite often the pain is localized in the big toe. The disease is caused when the body produces more uric acid than the kidneys and bladder are able to eliminate. The excess uric acid crystalizes and gathers in the joints producing redness and swelling. The stool allows the affected foot to be elevated to a comfortable height and angle to offer relief from the aching pain.

The museum artifact is made from solid hard wood with a dark finish. It was probably produced in the late nineteenth or early twentieth century. The stool is ten and a half inches wide and eighteen inches tall when erected. The design allows the stool to be folded for transportation or storage, and is height adjustable. These therapeutic devices were most popular during the eighteenth and nineteenth centuries.

Gout was considered the "rich man's" disease as those who contracted it could afford copious amounts of red meat, mushrooms, shell fish, plus a large amount of alcohol. Many notable people were claimed as victims of this disease, to include: Benjamin Franklin, Thomas Jefferson, John Milton, and even King Henry VIII of England!

Dazey Butter Churn made between 1910—1917

The Dazey Butter Churn

Most everyone recognizes the old fashioned butter churns in the display areas dedicated to the early settlers, but atop the display of items from the Brown Dixon Mercantile store is a very unique item. It's a metal butter churn that was made between 1910 and 1917 by the Dazey Churn and Manufacturing Company of St. Louis, Missouri. These churns were much faster and easier to use than the traditional butter churn. In 1904, E. B. Jones developed a glass churn with wooden paddles and gained the financial support of Nathan Dazey for its production. Dazey bought out his partner and the company eventually became the most prolific US maker of butter churns, both in glass (more numerous) and metal (as on display in the museum). Churns were produced from 1906 until the mid-1950s. World War I was a boon to the company as a butter shortage existed due to war demands. With the combined advent of electric refrigerators which greatly extended the life of butter reducing the need of frequent production, and the large migration of farmers to urban areas, the churn slowly lost its appeal. During World War II, Dazey mainly manufactured electric can openers and 20mm shells for the war effort. In the 1950s large companies took up butter production and Dazey churns became collector's items.

German Army Helmet
Made in World War I
Repurposed for World War II

German WWI "Stahhelm" Military Helmet

This helmet was "liberated" at Normandy on D-Day, June 6, 1944, by an American soldier from Jacksonville, Texas. Initially it was thought to be a WWII era helmet, but close examination revealed it to be of 1917 or 1918 WWI vintage. This style helmet replaced the spiked German Imperial Army type made of leather. The new version helmet first saw action during the Battle of Verdun in 1916. Head injuries were greatly reduced by its adoption. Note the two "lugs" on each side of the helmet. These created improved ventilation and allowed an additional piece of armor to be added at the front. The "stahlhelm" (steel helmet) continued to be revised throughout both WWI and WWII. It is one of the most iconic and successful helmets in military history. Today's modern NATO forces wear a similar appearing headgear.

J.L. Brown Store, Commerce St, 1917

Spring Shopping 1922

A hundred years ago, when spring was in the air in Jacksonville, many in town would visit local merchants to purchase a spring wardrobe or perhaps a new piece of furniture or farm equipment. Two of the most popular were the Brown Dixon Store and its chief competitor, S. H. Ragsdale.

One review of the Brown Dixon store states,

"The charming window display of goods in this store attract to the interior, where the order and general neatness are evidence that the groceries for sale here are of pure quality, the butter not filled with the flavor of tobacco, nor the sugar with kerosene. These pleasant surroundings further indicate that prompt and genteel attention will be given the customer."

Here is a list of Do's and Don'ts published in the 1922 Jacksonville Progress.

"Purchasers should, as far as possible, patronize the merchants of their own town. It is poor policy to send money abroad for articles which can be bought as cheaply at home."

"Do not take hold of a piece of goods which another is examining. Wait until it is replaced upon the counter before you take it up."

"Injuring goods when handling, pushing aside other persons, lounging upon the counter, whispering, loud talk and laughter, when in a store, are all evidences of ill-breeding."

"Never attempt to "beat down" prices when shopping. If the price does not suit, go elsewhere. The just and upright merchant will have but one price for his goods, and he will strictly adhere to it."

"It is an insult to a clerk or merchant to suggest to a customer about to purchase that he may buy cheaper or better elsewhere. It is also rude to give your opinion, unasked, about the goods that another is purchasing."

Above - Clapp Dixon Store
Below - Gillespie's Variety Store, Commerce St—1921

Spring Shopping 1922 - continued

"Never expect a clerk to leave another customer to wait on you; and, when attending upon you, do not cause him to wait while you visit with another. When the purchases are made let them be sent to your home, and thus avoid loading yourself with bundles."

"Treat clerks, when shopping, respectfully, and give them no more trouble than is necessary. Ask for what is wanted, explicitly, and if you wish to make examination with a view to future purchase, say so. Be perfectly frank. There is no necessity for practicing deceit."

"The rule should be to pay for goods when you buy them. If, however, you are trusted by the merchant, you should be very particular to pay your indebtedness when you agree to. By doing as you promise, you acquire habits of promptitude, and at the same time establish credit and make reputation among those with whom you deal."

"It is rude in the extreme to find fault and to make sneering remarks about goods. To draw unfavorable comparisons between the goods and those found at other stores does no good, and shows want of deference and respect to those who are waiting on you. Politely state that the goods are not what you want, and, while you may buy, you prefer to look further."

"If a mistake has been made whereby you have been given more goods than you paid for, or have received more change than was your due, go immediately and have the error rectified. You cannot afford to sink your moral character by taking advantage of such mistakes. You should do as you would be done by. Permanent success depends upon your being strictly honest."

Perhaps life today might be a little less stressful if our fellow shoppers, both in store and on line, followed these simple rules of good behavior.

The Sound of His Master's Voice 1922

The Victrola Talking Machine

The Vanishing Texana Museum was gifted a 1922 Model W 260 Victrola record player. This was a product of the Victor Talking Machine Company of Camden, New Jersey. There were three versions of this particular model, the last being produced in 1925. The wooden cabinet is constructed of walnut, though mahogany was an alternate and oak was added three years later. There were 53,683 Model W 260 manufactured, of which the museum's example is number 6,828.

This machine was hand powered by a crank linked to a two-spring motor. No electricity was involved, as the sound was projected by acoustic energy which vibrated a diaphragm and was broadcast by an internal metal horn. The speed of the record was hand adjustable. In 1923, the original cost was $150. Importantly, the former unsightly external horn had been replaced with an internal one changing the cabinet into a piece of desirable household furniture.

The term "Victrola" applies only to horn phonographs made by the Victor Talking Machine Company. Eldridge Reever Johnson (1867- 1945) founded the Victor Company in 1901, after training as a machinist and being told he was "too dumb to go to college." Though it was Thomas Edison who invented the cylinder phonograph, it was Johnson's company that mastered the flat record disk which won over the market.

Victor's acumen for advertising and marketing claimed a giant share of the phonograph and record market prior to 1925. Johnson signed numerous stars, such as opera notable Enrico Caruso, to exclusive recording contracts. Between 1906 and 1929, Johnson's company produced over eight million records! Victor talking machines became standard in almost every upper and middle-class home in America and Western Europe.

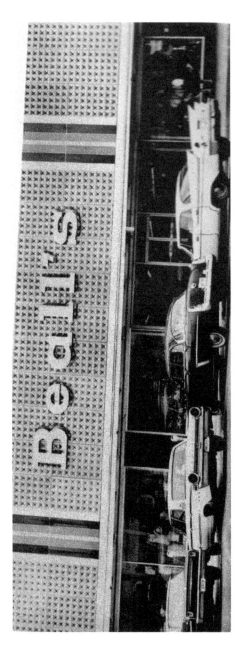

Beall's Department Store 1923

The 3 Beall's Brothers

In 1923, three brothers, Archie, Willie, and Robbie Beall, opened a small dry goods store in Henderson, TX. Their motto was *"Quality merchandise at reasonable prices, with one price to all."* This motto of being fair businesspersons would be the basis of their growth and success.

When the Great Depression hit, they were active in purchasing other dry good stores that had not been as careful with their operations. By 1930, Bealls had grown to seven stores. It was that year that the brothers bid on purchasing two retail stores, one in Tyler and the former J.L. Douglas Dry Goods store in Jacksonville. They won the bid for the Jacksonville store. Records indicate the business was located in "the old Mayfield building" which we think is currently the new Jacksonville Pubic Library.

There was a second floor to the building and so the home office of the Beall Brothers stores was moved to Jacksonville. They remained there until 1936 when they moved to 118 East Commerce Street the current location of the Treasure Cove Antique Mall. If you visit Treasure Cove, you will still see the Beall's name at the entrance. Bealls corporate offices were located upstairs.

By 1957 the company had grown to 38 stores. That year they moved their headquarters and warehouse operations to a new location on "the Henderson Highway." By the time of the Jacksonville Centennial there were 61 stores, 60 in Texas

The 1980's were some of the toughest economic times Texas had ever seen and the economy suffered a major contraction. In 1988, corporate officers Royce and Ray Beall announced plans to sell the company. The Beall stores were combined with the Palais Royal Stores in Houston to form a new company that would eventually become the Stage Stores. In 2019 Jacksonville's Stage Store on South Jackson Street was closed and other stores were grouped under the Gordon's Store name.

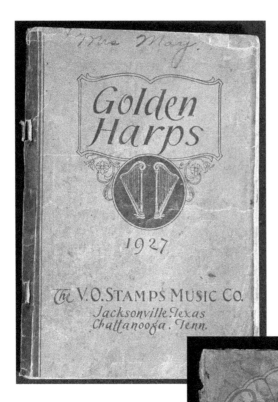

**V.O. Stamps Music
Company 1927**

When the Saints Come Marching In

At the 2021 Flag Day Celebration, a young group from the Sweet Union Baptist Church played a rousing rendition of the song, "When the Saints Come Marching In." According to Wikipedia, in 1937, Luther G. Presley composed words for the song based on an African American spiritual song. It was his boss, Virgil O. Stamps, who wrote the accompanying music to the words. Before that, in 1924, V.O. Stamps started his music company right here in Jacksonville, TX.

Virgil was born in Upshur County, TX. His love for music eventually leads him to be hired around 1917 by the Vaughn Publishing Company to open a sales office here in Jacksonville. Mr. Vaughn is generally considered to be a principal founder of Southern Gospel Music.

Ever the promoter, Stamps feels the East Texas thirst for fresh gospel music is being unfulfilled and so in 1924 he founded the V.O. Stamps School of Music here in Jacksonville. His first gospel music book, Harbor Lights, is a success, so much so that he asks his friend, J. R. Baxter, to become his music partner. In 1927, they change the name of the company to the Stamps-Baxter Music and Publishing Company and two years later move the headquarters to Dallas where resources that are more musical are available to them.

The partners also establish the Stamps Gospel Quartet. In fact, they authorize 11 groups to use that name including the Stamps-Baxter Blackwood Brothers. In Dallas, a local radio station picks up on their music and broadcasts a regular show. In those days, AM radio stations could power up during the late evening hours extending their reach, and therefore the influence of Stamps-Baxter Music, into the entire midwest. Stamps-Baxter becomes the premier publisher and entertainment resource for gospel music. Even Elvis records an album with the Stamps-Baxter Quartet. Virgil dies in 1940, so Baxter returns to Dallas to head up the business. After his death, ownership passes to various corporations.

Pay Phones Circa 1925

Call Me!

Our museum hosts a quality collection of antique and collectable telephones. Two of the phones are pay phones, almost a relic in today's world of cell phones. The oldest pay phone still has its original advertisement, "DON'T WRITE. TALK!" and instructions for use starting with "Have your nickel ready!"

By the 1880's phones were becoming a key component of American life. A need was recognized to have phones in locations other than for private use in homes and business. Local telephone agents would allow customers to use their phones and then pay a fee following the call. To assure payment many agents would lock the callers in a small booth, unlocking it only after payment was made through a slot in the door. The story goes that a Mr. William Gray asked to use an agent's phone to call a doctor for his ailing wife, was denied several times, and so the idea of a public phone had been seeded in his mind.

His solution was relatively simple. As a coin was deposited it would ring a bell on its way down into a locked coin box. An operator, listening in, could tell the value of the coins by the different tones of the bell and the number coins deposited by the number of times the bells rang. In 1889, the first payphone was installed in the Hartford Trust Company in downtown Hartford, CT. A model that would become the standard for pay phones, the Model 50A payphone, was installed in New York City in 1911. The phones were a huge success. Western Electric ramped up production and 24 months later there were over 25,000 payphones installed in the city.

By 1996, there were over 2,600,000 payphone, so naturally, they became part of our pop culture. Where would Superman have changed if there were no payphone booths? How would Melanie have escaped those flocks of gulls in Alfred Hitchcock's "The Birds?" Who can forget Maxwell Smart (Agent 86) entering a phone booth to access "CONTROL" headquarters or the payphone mounted on a wall with all the phone numbers of Fonzie's girlfriends written on it. Today there are less than 100,000 payphones. A "Calling From Your Car" phone booth is also on display in the museum.

Many Thanks to the Jolly Workers Club
1928

The Jolly Workers Club

S tanding in the city park near the museum is the World War I Dough Boy memorial statue, a part of the greater Cherokee County War Memorial. Originally this statue honored solely those Jacksonville American soldiers (of all colors) lost in WWI. Hostilities had concluded on November 11, 1918, a day then referred to as Armistice Day and now declared Veteran's Day. The task of raising the money for the statue was spearheaded by the Jolly Workers Club, an organization of twenty-four young working women in positions of responsibility around Jacksonville. In 1924, they contracted for the monument and raised $900 toward that end. The statue, carved by an unknown Italian sculptor and hewn from Italian Carrara marble, was completed and delivered. However, it was not erected as another $400 was needed for the inscription of names and erection costs.

In 1928, the Jacksonville Daily Progress ran a series of wrenching articles aimed at shaming the public and local government to obtain the needed funds for the statue's completion. One essay stated that the lack of completion "…stands as an accuser of tragic neglect on the part of the citizens of Jacksonville." Finally, the Chamber of Commerce and City Council got on board and checks and cash flowed so that needed funds were finally raised. The Dough Boy statue was erected on a plinth of Colorado marble and stood twelve feet high. The south-west corner of the City Park was selected as the location due to the high ground and two highway intersection. The statue depicts a uniformed soldier holding a Springfield 1903 (30-06) model rifle. He wears a hip length coat with artillery belt, a helmet, and ankle puttees. On three sides of the base are inscribed names of thirty-two fallen Jacksonville soldiers.

The inauguration day for the statue memorial was April 15, 1928, a beautiful Sunday, at 3:30 PM. It was a grand affair with bands playing and speeches given. The high point came when Mrs. T. M. Clairborne—the Gold Star mother of Jimmie W. Clairborne—the first Jacksonville soldier to fall, unveiled the statue.

In 1992, the original WWI monument of 1928, was transferred to a new location in the park and rededicated as the Cherokee County War Memorial.

United Gas System Service Vehicle

Natural Gas Service Arrives in Jacksonville

At 7:00 PM on January 19, 1928, a large crowd gathered around the band stand at the Northeast end of City Park to participate in a historic event. After a rousing selection of songs played by a Cornet Band, plus speeches from local politicians, an automobile procession began to form. The line of cars wound its way over to the Tyler Highway (now US 69) then looped back to a point where the new natural gas main crossed the highway into Jacksonville. At 8:00 PM, while the assembled crowd cheered and the brass band played, the valve to allow the flow of natural gas into Jacksonville was opened. The gas flowed into a 2" gas pipe, open at the top that ran up some 40' into the air. Gus Blankenship, then president of the Chamber of Commerce, hoisted, via a temporary flag pole, a blazing rag into the air. When it reached the natural gas flowing out of the top of the pipe, a huge blue explosion, some 40' in diameter, mushroomed atop the open pipe. Natural gas service provided by the Dixie Gas and Fuel Company had arrived in Jacksonville.

The following day installation of the gas meters began. Dixie and 50 other companies were acquired in 1930 to form the United Gas System and Jacksonville was selected to be the headquarters.

In 1968 the Pennzoil Corporation purchased United Gas System. At the time of its takeover United operated the busiest pipeline network in the United States, carrying 8% of the nation's supply, and was eight times the size of Pennzoil! The dramatic takeover, accomplished by a cash tender offer using vast amounts of borrowed money and United's own assets as collateral, was the first of its kind in the United States. This led to a wave of corporate raiders that still roam the business landscape today. Today, ATMOS Energy is Jacksonville's natural gas distributor.

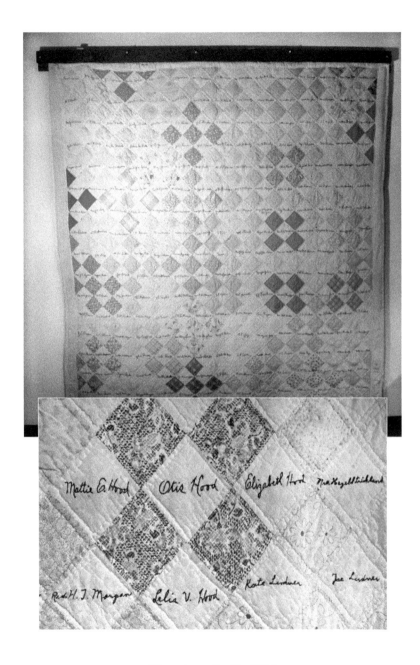

Signature Quilt 1932

Money Making Quilts

The Cove Springs Methodist Church began to organize in the 1850's just before the Civil War. Cove Springs itself is a small unincorporated community located just off US Highway 175 between Jacksonville and Frankston, Texas. In the year 1932, East Texas was experiencing, along with the rest of the nation, the Great Depression. The church in Cove Springs needed repairs and funds were short. It was decided that the church community would make quilts as a fund raiser for the needed church improvements. On one quilt white squares would be sold for ten cents upon which each contributor's name would be hand embroidered with black thread. Alternate various colored print squares - blue, green, and reddish pink - were added offsetting the family names. Total squares purchased numbered 239. Each name was hand stitched into the fabric of the quilt. Ethel Holcomb Hood designed and created this historic quilt now located at the museum. Also, her daughter, Mrs. Elsie Hood, won the popularity contest that year, at one cent per vote, and therefore received the completed quilt. The sale of the signature quilt along with the other quilts raised $800 for the Cove Springs Methodist Church.

In 1984, the Hood family, after years of loving use, returned the celebrated quilt again to the church for an additional fund raiser lottery. Prior to the event, Mrs. Bob Tipton made the necessary repairs to the binding. Donations were collected and a drawing was held. The quilt's winner was Mrs. Roy D. Adams. She gifted the quilt again to the church to be placed in the fellowship hall for viewing, and there it remained for many years. Numbers of recognizable family names from the area are present on the quilt. Indeed, all the names are legible except one. Perhaps they failed to pay for their spot as promised? Some of the families listed are: Acker, Barber, Brown, Devereaux, Hood, Holcomb, Tower (the mother of the late Senator John Tower), and many other familiar names.

Janice Jarratt   1934

Our Texas Queen

In 1934, Sam and C.D. Jarratt, founders of Jacksonville's "Tomato Deal" organized a pageant called "Romance of the Love Apple" to promote their crop. A key attraction was Janice Jarratt, C.D.'s. daughter. Now Janice was not just another pretty face asked to ride a float. At the time she was the "most photographed woman in the world!" Janice was the "Sweetheart (Queen) of the Texas Centennial" held in 1936. Our local Jacksonville gal hosted and oversaw every event honoring the 100th anniversary of the founding of the Texas Nation.

 For the following three years she was recognized as the "Number One Photographers' Model in the United States." Her fame at the Texas Centennial won her a trip to Los Angeles via American Airlines and the attention of the Hollywood studios. Although she returned to Texas, she was soon aboard the Southern Pacific railroad returning to Los Angeles. Her arrival was announced in the entertainment section of the August 17th Los Angeles Times with the headline, " Sweetheart of Texas Arrives for Film Debut." She did star in films like "Kids Millions" and "When Love Is Young", but soon her star started to fade. In March of 1937, she announced her engagement to "G-man" Melvin Pervis. Purvis had become famous for leading the manhunts that captured bank robbers such as Baby Face Nelson, John Dillinger, and Pretty Boy Floyd. Purvis became the FBI's golden boy, having captured more of designated public enemies than any other agent, but found himself sidelined after he began to enjoy better press than J. Edgar Hoover. Sadly for Melvin, Janice stood him up at a Hollywood prenuptial party and he returned to San Francisco to practice law.

Janice's Hollywood star eventually burned out. She marries Thomas Deely and then Alfred Urban Morrison moving to San Antonio, TX where she passes on September 29, 1991.

Champions Trophy

The Pickers and Jaxs

On the evening of July 12, 1917, the first professional baseball team to call Jacksonville home was formed.- The Jacksonville Tomato Pickers. The Pickers played in the East Texas League but only for one year. It would be 1934 before another professional baseball team called Jacksonville home - the Jacksonville Jax. The games were usually played at Highland Park field (located near what would be the future site of the Tomato Bowl and north of the railroad tracks). During their history the Jacksonville Jax were affiliated with several big league teams including the New York Giants, St. Louis Cardinals, Cleveland Indians, and Dallas Rebels.

Two signed baseballs and other memorabilia from that era are on display. The oldest is a National League game ball of the 1935 Jacksonville Jax then competing in the West Dixie League. This ball was signed by players and managers, and several were future big leaguers. Ford C. Frick was the sixth National League president at this time and his name is also embossed on the ball. Mr. Frick will become the Commissioner of Baseball in 1951 serving until 1965. Frick was president (sixth) of the National League from 1934 till 1951, and then elected Commissioner of Baseball for both leagues.

Several interesting characters were members of this 1935 team. One was Japhet Monroe "Red" Lynn (1913-1977). Red pitched in the major league from 1939 through 1944, with the Chicago Cubs, Detroit Tigers and New York Giants. During the off season he worked as a pro boxer, wrestler, rodeo cowboy, and railroad brakeman! In 1937, he won 32 games losing 13, with 233 strike outs. In that same year, Red led the East Texas League in both ERA and games pitched. He left the Jacksonville Jax in 1939 for the big leagues joining the Detroit Tigers. Red was a Texas boy out of Kenning.

Jacksonville Jax 1947

The Pickers and Jaxs - Continued

In addition to Red Lynn, of the nineteen players listed on the 1935 Jax team, five made it to the major leagues: Johnnie "Tip" Tobin (appeared in only one major league ballgame with the New York Giants), Ray Cunningham (St. Louis Cardinals), Al Unser (catcher, and but one of several from his family to reach the major leagues), and Herman Franks. Mr. Franks was the most successful of all the Jacksonville Jax. He played catcher, was the right hand man of Leo Durocher with Brooklyn Dodgers, a team mate of Jackie Robinson, a mentor of Willie Mays, and manager of the San Francisco Giants for four years.

The second signed baseball in the museum is the 1950 league championship ball of the Jacksonville Jax. Accompanying this is a large color photograph of team members and their championship trophy.

The trophy reads: "Jacksonville Jax, Presented to Play Off Champions, Gulf Coast League, 1950, Howard L. Green, President, President's Award." The Jax throughout their history had won three previous league championships in 1934, 1935, and 1937. The 1950 title was their fourth. It will also be their last as 1950 was the final year of the Jax.

Your Vanishing Texana Museum

Our Largest Artifact

Jacksonville's museum building is our largest artifact! The museum is located in the City Park, and was originally Jacksonville's first library. A local bond issue in 1936 combined with federal funding through President Franklin D. Roosevelt's Works Progress Administration (WPA), produced the $20,000 needed to complete the project. The iconic building was completed in 1940 and officially opened in 1941.

Sidney William Ray (1878-1954) was the architect, and pinkish-brown stone from a quarry near Alto, Texas, was the primary building material. Mr. Ray also designed the old City Hall, a fire station, and an old mill in the Jacksonville area. In recent years, an original pen and ink sketch of the building drawn by the architect was gifted to the Vanishing Texana Museum by Ms. Shirley Scown, granddaughter of Mr. S.W. Ray.

The structure was enlarged in the 1960s, thanks to J.L. Brown, a benefactor. In 2012, all museum items were relocated back to the old stone building. This move followed a $50,000 renovation doubling the previous space for the museum. Although the museum utilizes most of the building's space, the site also accommodates the City Senior Center and Meals on Wheels. Importantly for the museum is that it finally has a city provided curator. A Board of Directors of local citizens advises and assists the curator.

This building and its contents are one of the crown jewels of Jacksonville in this 2022 Sesquicentennial celebratory year!

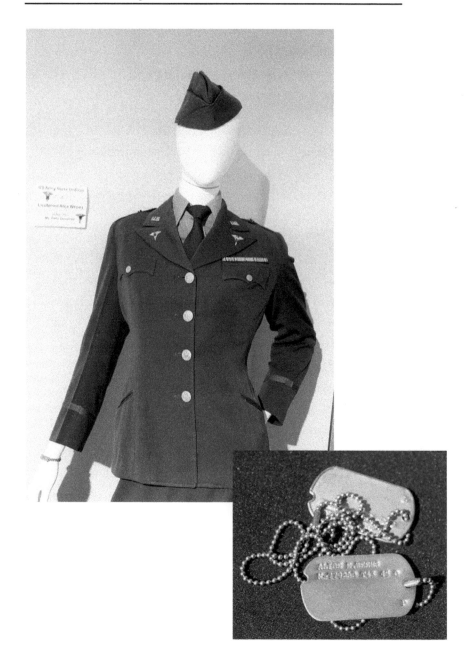

Lt. Alice Weems U.S. Army 1942

Nurse Officer Uniform of WWII

Female officer WWII uniforms are relatively rare. The VT Museum was gifted the winter uniform of Army nurse Lt. Alice E. Weems by her niece, Patty Crenshaw, former Jacksonville resident and city employee. Alice Weems graduated from the Shreveport School of Nursing on May 12, 1942. She completed her basic training at the Brooke General Hospital at Fort Sam Houston near San Antonio and was then shipped to the Pacific theater. There she served on several islands shortly after they were captured by US Marines. Her hospital units treated wounded from Iwo Jima, Okinawa, and Tinian. She was serving on Tinian Island, in the Mariana chain, when the B-29 Super Fortress the Enola Gay was launched from Tinian and dropped the Atomic bomb on Hiroshima. Her last assignment was at war's end in the Philippines where she attended the war crime trail of General Yomoyuki Yamashita, the infamous "Beast of Bataan".

Along with her Class-A winter uniform are associated items of Lt. Weems, including dog tags, US Army identity card, and assorted uniform accoutrements such as badges and ribbons. The dog tags include her serial number, N 779260 T43 45 O. The "N" represents "nurse". The 779260 is her official serial number, and the 45 indicates the year she received her tetanus and tetanus toxoid shots. The "O" identifies blood type. The bottom "P" represents Lt. Weem's Protestant religious preference. Weem's tags are type 3 (July, 1943 through March, 1944). The well-known notch in the metal tags allowed the tag to be positioned on the embossing machine for stamping, and was unofficially used to set in the mouth of deceased soldiers for future identification.

The left side of the coat displays three original service ribbons awarded to Lt. Weems: American Campaign Medal, American-Pacific Campaign Medal, and WWII Victory Medal. The two coat lapels each display the insignia pin of military nursing, a gold caduceus containing a large red "N" for nurse. Nurse Weems became a civilian nurse following the war. She died on October 4, 1999, and is buried in Marshall, Texas.

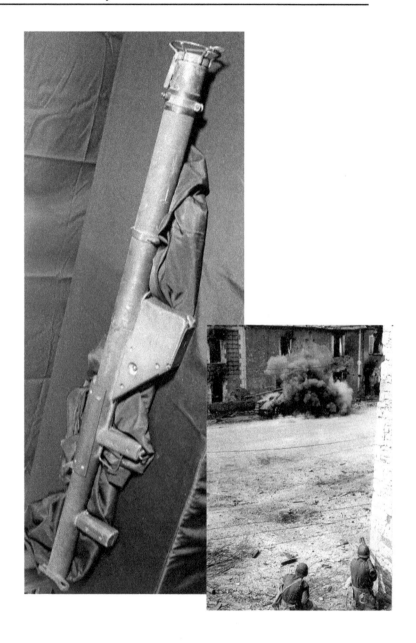

M-1 Bazooka
1942

A Loud Mouthed Bazooka

The M-1 Bazooka (official name: Launcher, rocket, 2.36 inch, Anti-Tank, M-1) was developed in 1942 by ordinance innovators Captain Leslie Skinner and Lt. Edward Uhl as an anti-tank weapon. They had the rocket but were unable to come up with a delivery system until Lt. Uhl was walking past the base dump and observed a pipe about the same size as the rocket-grenade. In an "eureka" moment he stated, "That's the answer! Put the tube on a soldier's shoulder with the rocket inside, and away it goes!"

The museum's bazooka was brought home from the war to Jacksonville, stowed in a closet and later gifted to our museum. It is a very early version of the bazooka. The length is 54.5 inches with serial number 9365. Two men operated the weapon, one to load and the other to fire. The bazooka got its nick name from a 1930s radio star, a comedic musician named Bob Burns who invented a novelty tubular horn he called a "bazooka." In Dutch dialect the word "bazooka" means "loud mouthed."

This weapon was a success on the battlefield against armored vehicles, machine gun nests, and fortified bunkers. General Dwight D. Eisenhower ranked it among the four most important "tools of victory" of WWII, along with the jeep, C-47 cargo plane, and Atom bomb!

After the war, in 1947, several GIs who used the bazooka in the Pacific returned to Staten Island, New York and established a new business product together– chewing gum. They named their new gum Bazooka, and the rest is history!

Jacksonville Jolter
1944

The J'ville Jolter

"The J'ville Jolter" (42-31634) was the only known warplane to be named after our community. Its first pilot was 1st Lt. Raymond R. Ward (1921-2003), a native of Jacksonville and graduate of Jacksonville High School. The nose art Ward chose for his aircraft depicted the JHS Indian Maiden with the nick name of his wife "Chubby" painted over the top, and "The J'ville Jolter" beneath. Raymond Ward eventually wrote his war memoirs entitled "My Experiences in WW II" (1998), which are featured in the Vanishing Texana Museum along with accompanying photographs.

At twenty-three years of age on, March 6, 1944, as part of the 8th Air Force - 91st Bomb Group, 322nd Squadron Leader Ward led his group on the first American daylight bombing of Berlin. He would complete 26 missions during the war. His last mission on March 24, 1944, was also to Berlin. Over the English Channel ack-ack from the Frisian Islands knocked out the number four engine which was quickly feathered (taken off line). Ward returned the plane safely to base with no casualties.

After Ray Ward returned to the States, "The J'ville Jolter" continued to fly combat missions and became the lead plane for the entire 91st Group. Unfortunately, the mission to bomb the aircraft factory in Halle, Germany, on 16 August, 1944, proved a disaster. Twenty-five German fighters attacked the group and in 30 seconds six American bombers were shot down. "The J'ville Jolter" was one of these. Pilot 1st Lt. Holstead Sherrill and four others were killed. One of those dying was Texan Enrique T. Perez, staff sergeant. Four additional crew members parachuted only to be captured and sent to POW camps. The aircraft made four spins and exploded in a ball of fire.

Paul Ragsdale 1945—2011

**Right— During
Legislative Session**

ums
to sax
is guitar
or sax

**At his happiest
with his band**

They Called Him "Rags!"

Paul Ragsdale was born the son of Simeon Virgil Ragsdale (1920-1957), a barber and Emmittee Arnwine (1922-2002). His parents lived in Mount Haven, a small community just west of Jacksonville. Both parents were descendents of local slaves that worked the cotton fields in Old Jacksonville. It was a challenge growing up during those transition years from segregation to integration, but Paul had parents, family, and church to encourage him to become his own person.

Following completion of junior high school in Mount Haven, Paul transferred to the segregated Fredrick Douglas High School where he excelled in academics and music. During his junior year he was president of the student council and superintendent of the Mount Haven Methodist Church.

The summer before his senior year was traumatic yet important to the man Paul would become. He and a friend were confronted and assaulted by a gang of older whites and beaten to the point of needing hospitalization. The offenders were verbally scolded and lightly fined. Worried for his future, his family sent him to Austin to live with relatives and finish high school.

Paul was accepted at the University of Texas where he majored in sociology. Although he was allowed to reside in a student dorm, he was denied use of the student cafeteria. Calling on his music background and membership in the orchestra, Paul applied for the UT Marching Band, but was not allowed to participate.

Following graduation with a BA degree in sociology in 1966, Paul stayed in Austin working for various government agencies, but eventually moves to Dallas where he was employed by the Youth Opportunity Program. That summer, after being refused service at several public places, he files one of the first civil rights complaints in Dallas under the Civil Rights Act of 1964.

Paul finally jumps off into the world of politics and is immediately elected to the Texas House of Representatives for Dallas' Oak Cliff District 10. This was a political watershed as he was among the first Blacks elected to the legislature since Reconstruction. Space does not allow for a list of his many accomplishments during seven terms in office, but are part of his exhibit in the museum.

Paul returns to Jacksonville where in 1997 he marries Deborah Marie Oden. Paul continued to serve his community including service with the Jacksonville Independent School District. Paul died on August 14, 2011 following a stroke.

Wire Recorder
Sears, Roebuck, & Co.
1948

A Spool There Was

On display in the museum is a 1940's era Wire Recorder manufactured by the Sears & Roebuck Co.

The wire recorder was invented in 1898 by Valdemar Poluson, a Danish American. Poluson's US Patent, issued in 1898, calls his wire recorder a "Telegraphone." His patent consisted of a thin wire being rapidly pulled across a recording head. The head used electrical current to magnetize each point along the wire with the intensity and polarity of the audio signal being supplied. When the wire was later pulled back across a similar recording head (that is not electrified), the varying magnetic field on the wire will induce a similar magnetic field, thereby recreating the original signal. The standard speed of the wire was 24 inches per second. The wire was as thin as a human hair, so over a mile of wire would fit on a standard 3" diameter spool.

With the outbreak of World War II, the need for a secure, durable, and more portable recording device became apparent. Their most famous use was by Navajo code talkers who recorded secured messages to be sent to other Navajo code talkers who would then translate them.

A wire recorder, disguised as a sewing box, was used by Hogan's Heroes to record a meeting in Kommandant Klink's office. A wire recorder was also the subject of a 1966 episode of Mission Impossible entitled "A Spool There Was."

Wire recorders references still linger in our language – "wiretap," "on the wire," and "wired for sound" - all have their basis in the 1898 invention of Valdemar Poulsen.

**POEMS
WRITTEN
IN A
NORTH KOREA
P.O.W. CAMP
1950 - 1953**

**James Raymond Wells
POW—North Korea
1950**

"THE SIXTEEN HUNDRED"

Not a bugle was heard, not a funeral beat,
Nor even a drum sounding retreat,
As over the ice the corpses were carried,
To the hill where those "GI's" are buried.

Six foot by two foot by one foot deep,
On a Korean hillside they sleep,
Young and old — all wondering why,
"Sixteen Hundred" had to die.

No little white crosses with their names,
But they are not buried in shame;
Although they lie in unknown graves,
"Sixteen Hundred," American braves.

No useless casket enclosed their breast,
"G.I." clothing for their last rest,
All colors of men; blacks, browns, and whites,
"Sixteen Hundred," faded lights.

A pill, a powder, medicine of any kind,
Or, should we say a stronger mind;
Could have saved them from yonder hill,
"Sixteen Hundred," laying still.

In their illness, tossing and turning,
Most of them knew there would be no returning,
Some went easy, some with pain,
"Sixteen Hundred," died in vain.

When we go home to enjoy our fill,
They are there still on that lonely hill,
Forgotten by some, remembered by most,
"Sixteen Hundred," in their last post.

James Raymond Wells
POW Camp 5 - North Korea

The Korean War had its roots in 1910 when Japan annexed Korea as part of its imperial plan to control all of Asia that led to the bombing of Pearl Harbor. After World War II the allies divided Korea in half at the 38th parallel. After just 57 months, North Korea launched across the border into South Korea. The Koreans tried to resist, but the US Army, at the direction of the United Nations, entered the war. As far as the American government was concerned, this was a war against the forces of international communism whose goal was the destruction of democracy. After some back and forth movement across the 38th parallel, the war began to stall. Americans were not anxious to start a third world war against Russia and China, and so began to try and find a way to resolve the conflict.

Finally, on July 27, 1953, after the death of some 5,000,000 soldiers and civilians, an armistice was signed. No peace treaty was ever agreed to and so the problem persists.

During the three years of battle, some 7,245 American soldiers were captured and held as prisoners of war. One was a local Jacksonville resident, James Raymond Wells. James was captured and held for 33 months in the notorious P.O.W. Camp No. 5. While incarcerated James and his friends wrote, on small scraps of paper, poems about their experiences. James collected all he could and publishes them in a small booklet on display in the museum.

When James returned to Jacksonville, he began a career with the Jacksonville Daily Progress. The Daily Progress continues to honor him by flying the P.O.W. – M.I.A. flag over their building.

To the Moon and Back
November 1969

The Moon Over Jacksonville

This Texas flag was carried to the surface of the moon by Intrepid lunar pilot Astronaut Alan L. Bean (1932-2018) on November 19, 1969. Captain Bean and Mission Commander Charles "Pete" Conrad were the third and fourth person to land on the moon. Alan Bean carried this Texas flag inside his space suit for the seven- and one-half hours he was on the surface at the Ocean of Storms. Richard F. Gordon (module pilot) remained in the spacecraft orbiting the moon. Also, Alan Bean was the first Texan to walk on the moon.

Later, Astronaut Bean and his wife Sue Ragsdale Bean, formerly of Jacksonville, Texas, presented the flag to the Vanishing Texana Museum in memory of her parents, Mr. and Mrs. A. N. Ragsdale, both lifelong residents of Jacksonville. The border around the flag contains the signatures of the Apollo 12 crew, all now deceased.

Splash down was November 14, 1969, in the South Pacific. The all-Navy crew was picked up safely by the carrier the USS Hornet. Bean will later (1973) command the Skylab II mission and orbited earth for 59 days doing scientific research. Alan Bean later retired from NASA (1981) and devoted full time to art, painting a record of space exploration. He was a graduate of the University of Texas at Austin and is buried in the Arlington National Cemetery.

Mayor Acker
Memorial in front of museum

Jacksonville's Longest Serving Mayor

A white marble stela on the grounds of the Vanishing Texana Museum memorializes Mr. Tom E. Acker, the city's longest serving mayor. The top of the stone resembles an open book, and there an inscription states "Honoring T.E. Acker" with accomplishments on four sides. Members of the extended Acker family settled as early as 1848 in the Old Jacksonville area. Tom Acker (1890-1972) arrived in Jacksonville to attend Alexander College (later Lon Morris) in 1907. He met Miss Virginia "Virgie" Beard (1893-1987) there and they married in 1911. Tom specialized in business at school, and his first job was as secretary to the superintendent of the Texas and New Orleans Railway office. Next, he became secretary to the president of Jacksonville's First National Bank.

Mr. Acker entered public service when elected mayor of Jacksonville in 1919. He will serve in that position for thirty-three years until 1953. Tom served his city in other ways too. He was on the board of the First Methodist Church, taught Sunday School on a radio station KEBE broadcast, and was president of the Texas Bankers Association (1949-1950). Tom Acker's profession was that of banker, and in 1932 he became president of the Texas Bank and Trust.

Tom Acker was the face of Jacksonville for many years and through many events. Acker was instrumental in planning and carrying out the 1922 Jacksonville fiftieth founding celebration. He gave a speech in 1928 when the Jacksonville WWI War Memorial was inaugurated. Tom was mayor during the Great Depression and turbulent years of World War Two. Perhaps it is symbolic that he died (May 25) in 1972, the very year his city celebrated the hundredth anniversary of its founding in 1872. Tom and Virginia Acker are buried at Resthaven Cemetery in Jacksonville.

The World's Greatest Whistler

1984

The World's Greatest Whistler

Fred Lowery (1909-1984) was once introduced by Bob Hope as the "greatest whistler in the world", and the title stuck. Later Bob's buddy, Bing Crosby requested whistling lessons from Lowery. During his life, Fred worked with great stars such as Steve Allen, Edgar Bergen, Jackie Gleason, Ed Sullivan, and Judy Garland. In addition, he performed at Carnegie Hall and the White House for President Roosevelt (1937). He lived in Jacksonville and was blind!

Born near Palestine on November 2, 1909, At the age of two and the same year as his mother's death, he contracted scarlet fever which rendered him legally blind. Fred and siblings were raised by their grandparents on a farm near Jacksonville. Entering the Texas State School for the Blind in Austin at age ten in 1917, Fred developed his whistling skills and also studied piano, saxophone, violin, and voice. Finally, Lowery found professional whistling work in 1931 on the Dallas radio station WFAA's Early Birds. He appeared throughout the country during the late vaudeville period. In 1939, Fred Lowery recorded on Columbia Records "Indian Love Song", which sold almost 2,500,000 copies. In 1954, he recorded for MGM Records the unforgettable theme from the film "The High and the Mighty", which starred John Wayne. He also whistled the haunting melody theme in the film "The Proud Ones" in 1956, starring Robert Ryan and Virginia Mayo. During his career he would record eleven albums under various labels.

Fred Lowery married Grace Johnston of Jacksonville on December 20, 1940. They moved to Jacksonville to be near Grace's aging mother and lived on John Street. In 1983, Lowery published his autobiography *Whistling in the Dark*. The "King of the Whistlers" died on December 11, 1984. Fred and Grace are buried in the Jacksonville City Cemetery.

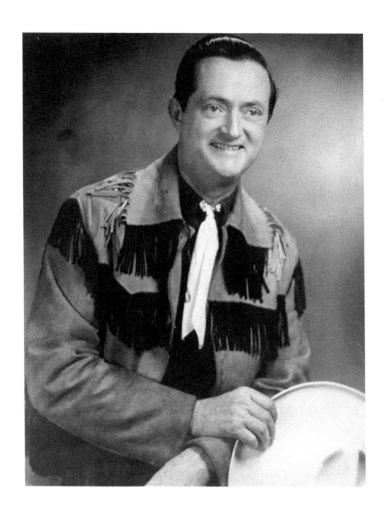

Al Dexter   1984

The Honky Tonk Man

Clarence Albert Poindexter was born on May 4, 1905, in Jacksonville, Texas, and evolved into a Country Music Hall of Fame inductee, a famed songwriter, and winner of twelve Gold Records. Dexter not only sang and wrote music, but also mastered the guitar, banjo, harmonica, organ and mandolin. His first recorded hit was a 1936 number entitled "Honky Tonk Blues," a song credited with introducing the term "honky tonk" into the country music vocabulary.

Dexter's iconic piece was "Pistol Packing Mama", which became one of the three bestselling records during WWII, selling three million copies. Numerous artists recorded the song, including Al Dexter, but it was Bing Crosby and the Andrew Sisters who made it a major hit in 1944. The unusual and comedic lyrics were inspired when a jealous woman waving a pistol entered a bar that Dexter operated searching for "the other woman". The lyrics emerged when Dexter asked himself what might one say to a woman in that situation. Incidentally, this number became the 1943 marching song of the New York Yankees!

Al Dexter is credited with influencing the musical style of both Merle Haggard and Glenn Campbell. He was inaugurated into the Nashville Songwriter's Hall of Fame in 1971, and the Texas Country Music Hall of Fame in Carthage, Texas, in 2010. In addition, he was the first country star to perform on Broadway.

Albert Poindexter (stage name Al Dexter) died on January 28, 1984 in Lewisville, Texas, and is buried nearby in Denton at the Roselawn Memorial Park.

Visiting Our Museum
The Vanishing Texana Museum is really two museums in one.

First, the museum hosts a large collection of items tied to the history of Jacksonville and its surrounding mircoplex. All items have been donated by local families and reflect not only the item themselves, but the often signs of hard work, struggles, and rewards these people lived for. The museum hopes that the reader of this book will consider donations of articles to the museum, rather than allow them to remain out of sight of those who will enjoy viewing and learning about them.

Secondly, the museum exhibits items on loan from private, local collectors. These are items visitors might never experience anywhere else. As always, we encourage anyone who has collected anything, no matter how small the collection, to contact the museum about how it might be exhibited to the enjoyment of our community. Currently there is no admission charge to visit the museum. Depending on the number of visitors, a docent may be available to take you on a guided tour, telling you the "backstory" on many items and assuring you will see all the highlights. There's even a special tour for the kids. The City of Jacksonville provides for the Vanishing Texana Museum's day-to-day operational expenses. Educational activities, special events, and exhibit as well as many other costs are covered by donations from people like you. Donations may be mailed to the Vanishing Texana Museum, 300 South Bolton, Jacksonville, TX 75766 or dropped off during a visit.

Please contact the museum if you wish to hold a special event during off hours.

About The Authors

Larry Lydick became the Curator of the Vanishing Texana Museum in 2016. Born in Southern California, he remained there until his marriage to Claudia Stallings of the Stallings family of New Summerfield, TX. After graduating with multiple degrees, including history and education, from Northern Arizona University, Mr. Lydick enjoyed a successful career primarily in the field of international lighting design and manufacturing. As past president of Sterner Lighting Systems, a Hubbell Company, as well as Director of Marketing and Sales for Fiberglass Specialties of Henderson, TX, Mr. Lydick was able to bring a variety of skills to his position with the museum. Many of you may have enjoyed his "Mysteries At Your Museum" series published in the local newspaper.

John Taylor was proudly born in Jacksonville, TX and attended elementary school there. He graduated from Woodrow Wilson High School in Dallas in 1957, and eventually earned a BS and M.Ed degrees at Texas A&M where he was a member of the Corps of Cadets. John is also a US Army Signal Corps veteran. For 30 years he taught overseas for the US Department of Defense in Libya, Germany, Bahrain, Spain, and Turkey. Retired, he is currently the chairperson of the board of the Vanishing Texana Museum.

CPSIA information can be obtained
at www.ICGtesting.com
Printed in the USA
BVHW021730240222
630016BV00011B/537